What Can We Do Today?

Written by Barbara Hojel and Ginger Guy

Illustrated by Linda Howard

 **LONGMAN**

Addison Wesley Longman

New York • London • Hong Kong

Copyright © 1999 by Addison Wesley Longman, Inc.
10 Bank Street, White Plains, NY 10606

ISBN: 0-201-35149-8

1 2 3 4 5 6 7 8 9 10-BAM-03 02 01 00 99

"I don't want to play at home today," said Michael.
"I want to ride in a boat."

"I want to ride on a train," said Joey.

"I want to fly in an airplane," said Erika.

"Do you know what I want to ride?" asked Mother. "I want to ride on a motorcycle!"

"But where can we ride in a boat, on a train, in an airplane, and on a motorcycle in one day?" asked Michael.

"I know just the place,"
said Father.
"We can get there on the bus."

"We can bring a picnic lunch,"
said Mother.

They rode the bus down many streets.
They saw many buildings.
They saw stores, restaurants, and offices.
Michael, Erika, and Joey waved at the cars,
taxis, and trucks.

"Here is the place," said Father.
"Come on."

"Where are we?" asked Joey.

"We're at the amusement park," said Father.

"I can ride in a boat!" said Michael.

"I can ride on a train!" said Joey.

8

"I can fly in an airplane!" said Erika.

"And I can ride on a motorcycle!" said Mother.

They rode in boats.
They rode on a train.
They flew in airplanes.
They rode on motorcycles.

"I'm hungry," said Father.
"Where's the picnic basket?"

"Oh, no!" said Mother.
"It's not here! Where is it?"

"Let's ride bicycles," said Joey.
"We can go look for our picnic basket."

"Good idea! I'm hungry, too," said Erika.

They went by the motorcycles,
but there was no picnic basket.
They went by the airplanes,
but there was no picnic basket.
They went by the train and boats,
but there was no picnic basket.

13

"Look!" said Michael. "There's our lunch."

"Oh no!" Mother said.
"Now we can't eat lunch."

"Yes, we can!" said Erika.
"I smell something good to eat!"

"I can smell it, too" said Joey.

15

"After lunch I want to ride on the motorcycles again!" said Mother smiling.